INDIAN LIFE IN PRE-COLUMBIAN NORTH AMERICA
Coloring Book

JOHN GREEN

Introduction and Captions by
Stanley Appelbaum

DOVER PUBLICATIONS, INC.
NEW YORK

Bibliographical Note

Indian Life in Pre-Columbian North America Coloring Book is a new work,
first published by Dover Publications, Inc., in 1994.

International Standard Book Number

ISBN-13: 978-0-486-28047-9
ISBN-10: 0-486-28047-0

Manufactured in the United States by RR Donnelley
28047009   2016
www.doverpublications.com

INTRODUCTION

The story of Native American life in North America (north of Mexico) is very complex and still full of unsolved problems. The present book tells the story very briefly and not completely, but by means of representative examples. It falls into two main parts, which are further subdivided.

The first half of the book (pages 4–25), based on archaeological findings, follows the career of human beings on the continent from their first entry (page 4), through the so-called Paleoindian period of big-game hunting (pages 5–7) and the Archaic period of food gathering, early farming and early village settlement (pages 8–11), into the later prehistoric period. This later period, in which there are many features of high civilization, is so varied that it is only represented here by three of the most significant and varied cultural areas: the Woodlands (the Northeast and Midwest), illustrated in the important Hopewell phase (pages 12 and 13) and Mississippian phase (pages 14–16); the Arctic (ancestors of the Inuit, pages 17 and 18); and the Southwest (ancestors of the Pueblo peoples, pages 19–25).

Scholars disagree on many points concerning the entire prehistoric period, particularly on dates; some dating theories have been very extreme indeed. For dating and similar technical matters, the present book follows the recent and highly reliable work *Ancient North America: The Archaeology of a Continent*, by Brian M. Fagan, published by Thames and Hudson, London and New York, in 1991.

The second half of the present book is a survey of various regions of North America as they were when the first Europeans reached those particular areas.* A number of the illustrations in this second half are based closely on the very first drawings or paintings ever made by European colonists or visitors; these are individually identified. The survey is arranged geographically in a way that to some extent also reflects the chronology of discovery: the Southeast (pages 26–31), the middle Atlantic coast (page 32), the Northeast (pages 33–36), the Great Lakes region (pages 37 and 38), the Plains (pages 39–41), the Great Basin (page 42), the Southwest (pages 43 and 44), California (page 45), the Northwest Coast (pages 46 and 47) and the Subarctic (page 48).

---

*Strictly speaking, "pre-Columbian" (as this book is titled) would mean "earlier than 1492," the year of Columbus' discovery, but it is here used loosely to mean (more or less) "up to the arrival of Europeans in any given area."

Northeast Asian hunters enter North America, about 12,000 B.C. Some fourteen or fifteen thousand years ago, when sea levels were very low because so much water had been trapped as ice, there was a broad stretch of dry land connecting the northeastern tip of Asia with Alaska, where the Bering Sea is now found. There was enough vegetation to support hardy animals such as mammoths and horses. Hunting parties of human beings entered North America from already populated Asia in pursuit of this game. More and more people arrived and ultimately spread throughout the Western Hemisphere over a considerable period of time, at first possibly following an ice-free corridor through Alaska and western Canada until reaching open territory. Some of the arrivals may even have been by boat between the two continents. The first people in North America (Paleoindians) probably wore clothing sewn from animal skins and were armed with simple spears tipped with stone.

Paleoindians attacking a trapped mammoth, about 9500 B.C.
Between eleven and twelve thousand years ago, the Clovis people (named for their long, fluted spear points first found near Clovis, New Mexico, in the 1930s) ranged all over North America. Although they surely ate small mammals, fish and plants as well, they were specialized in hunting very large animals (megafauna), such as giant bison, or mammoths trapped in bogs. Scientists still argue whether the disappearance of these animals around this time was due chiefly to overhunting, or whether climatic changes or other natural processes were more significant. The major kill sites of Clovis people have been found on the Plains and in the West of what is now the United States.

Later Paleoindians driving bison off a cliff, about 8000 B.C.
Later groups of hunters in the West, such as the Folsom people (named for another site in New Mexico), were especially hunters of bison (the modern species), which they would sometimes box in in a canyon or arroyo or even drive over cliffs. For example, the bones of about 120 animals have been found at the cliff site Bonfire Shelter in Texas. Similar spear points and tools from this time are found in widespread areas of North America, and there

was lively interregional trading in desirable types of stone. A number of Paleoindian cultures on the plains subsequent to the Folsom period are usually grouped together as "Plano"; their spear points were no longer fluted, and in general the quality of stoneworking was in decline.

Gathering berries and shellfish, about 5000 B.C. The period between 8000 and 1000 B.C. (the dates vary with geographical regions) is known as the Archaic. Within the first half of this period, although hunting remained important, people's diet became more varied as women gathered seeds, nuts and berries from wild plants, and fishing and shellfish gathering expanded.

Basketry became important as the need for containers developed. Duck decoys made of reeds are known from this era. Occupation of sites became more permanent and there was significant population growth. Beginning with the Archaic period, differences in life-styles became sharper between the various natural regions of North America, as local resources became more fully exploited.

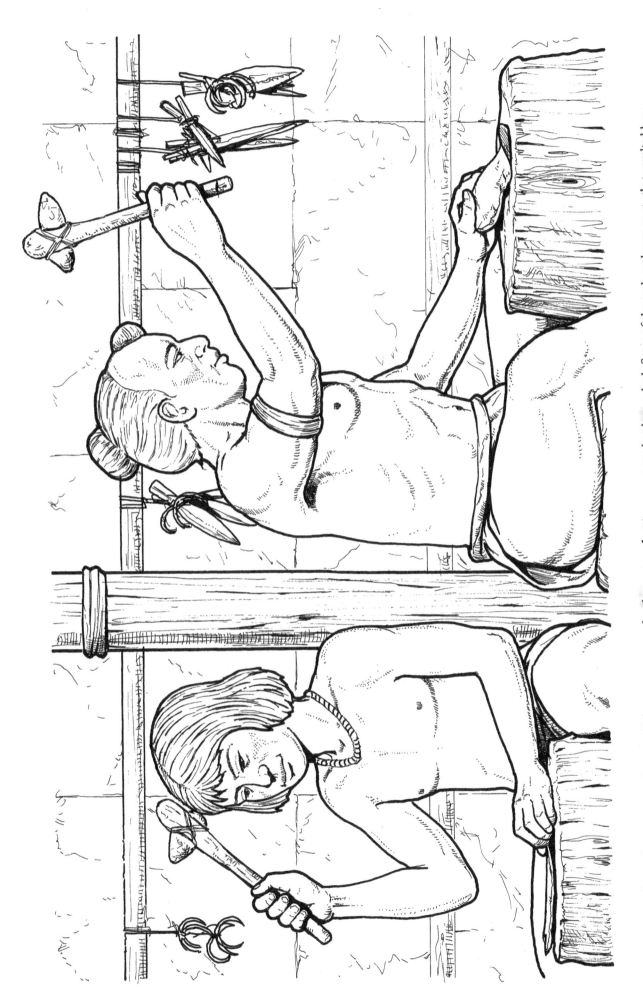

Men using stone tools to cold-hammer copper implements, about 3000 B.C. In the Great Lakes region, where there were exposed copper outcrops, simple metalworking was already practiced in the Late Archaic period. The metal could merely be picked up or very easily dug out and did not need to be smelted. Some of the tools and ornaments that resulted have been excavated thousands of miles from their source. Axe blades, gouges, fishhooks, beads and bracelets were manufactured in this way.

Primitive village scene in the Late Archaic. Further experience with wild plants led to the conscious raising of useful plants in small garden plots (horticulture); in this scene, tobacco is being grown. The need for improved containers for storage and cooking was met by the invention of simple pottery. These developments resulted in the establishment of permanent villages of hunter-gatherers. In some areas, such as the California coast, there was no further basic technological or social change until the coming of Europeans. Digging-sticks for unearthing tubers and grinding-stones for processing grain are other important tools of this period. The hunter in the foreground has a thrower device (atlatl) attached to his spear; this strengthens and extends the spear cast.

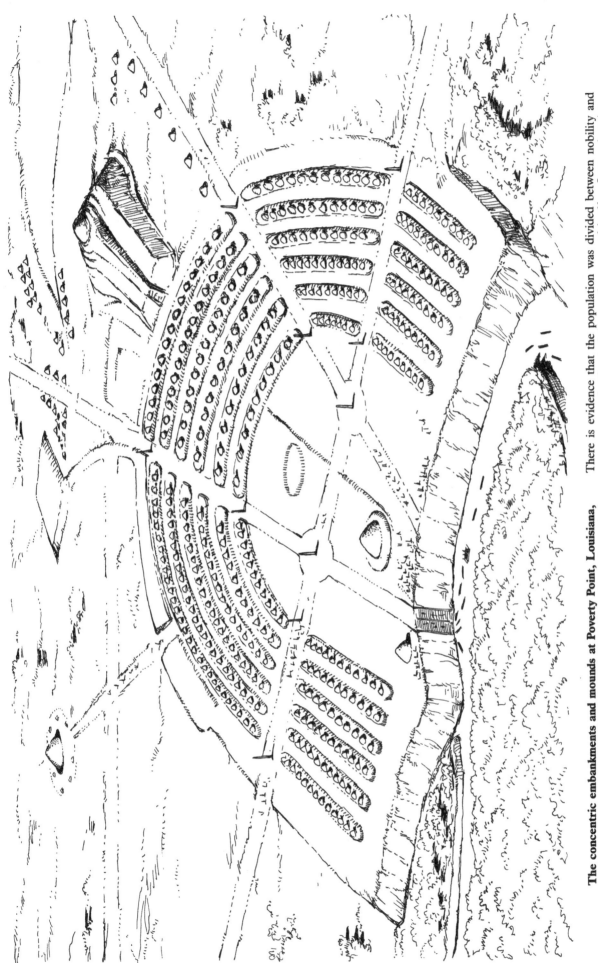

The concentric embankments and mounds at Poverty Point, Louisiana, about 1200 B.C. The Terminal Archaic, or Transitional, period (1500–1000 B.C.) witnessed the appearance of burial mounds and similar earth constructions in what is now the eastern half of the United States, which must imply a greater complexity in the organization of society. The largest mound on the Poverty Point site is about 70 feet high and 600 feet across.

There is evidence that the population was divided between nobility and commoners, both socially and geographically. Somewhat later (1000–100 B.C.) in the Early Woodland period of the Eastern and Midwest U.S., the Adena civilization in the Ohio River valley was characterized by hundreds of mounds, in some of which food and valuable objects were buried with the dead.

The Great Serpent Mound in Ohio, about 400 A.D. In the Middle Woodland period of eastern North America, about 200 B.C. to 400 A.D., the most notable culture is the Hopewell, named for a site in Ohio, and characterized by extensive mounds and enclosures. The core areas were located in Illinois and Ohio. The single most famous monument, located in Ohio, is the Great Serpent Mound, which runs 1,254 feet over a low ridge. The oval in the snake's jaws is a burial mound. The serpent may have been the totem of the clan buried there. Large permanent villages were a feature of the Illinois core area. Trade and exchange were well organized, and similar decorations are found on art works discovered in widely separated areas.

A Hopewell village with craftsmen at work. The artistic products of the Hopewell culture include some of the finest ever created in pre-Columbian North America. The standing man with the stone knife in his belt is holding a flat sculpture of the claws of a bird of prey made of sheet mica. His topknot hair style is known from statuary. Potters created not only the bowls shown, but also pipes and remarkable clay figurines. Sheet copper was formed into images, and figures of animals were made from many sorts of stone. Masks were made for shamans (medicine men) out of human skulls decorated with hides. The decline of this high culture has never been satisfactorily explained, but a change in climate (it grew much colder) may have contributed.

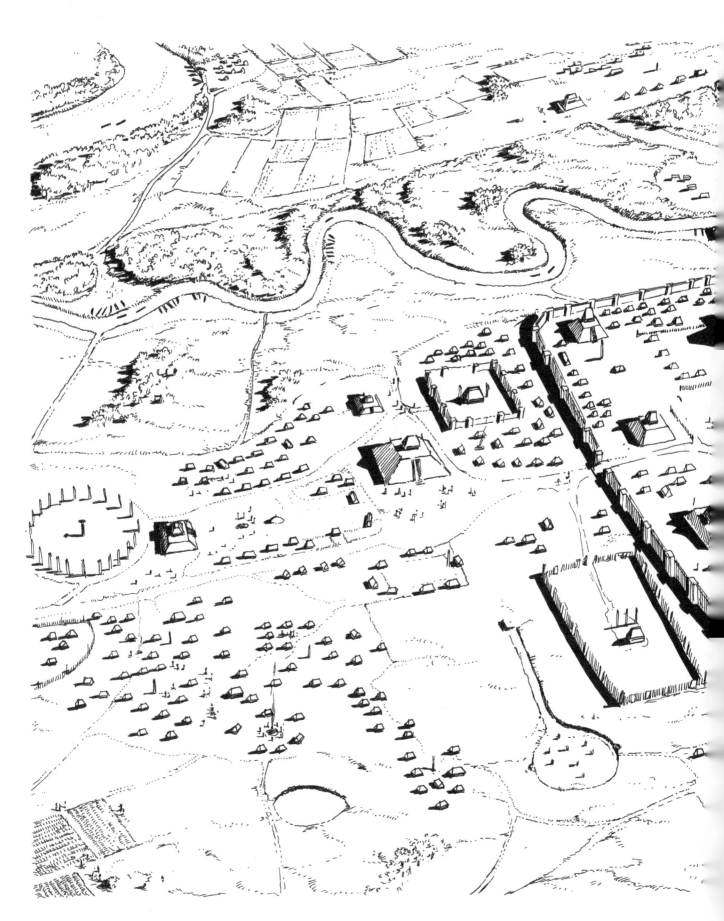

The major mounds at Cahokia, Illinois, about 1250 A.D. Between about 450 and 800 A.D., some peoples of the lower Mississippi valley built flat-topped platform mounds that were not meant for burials, but may have been substructures for temples or great houses. The grouping of such mounds around a plaza is one of the characteristics of the so-called Mississippian tradition of around 700 to 1500 A.D. The bow-and-arrow, not known in the area before about 500 A.D., now became common. Real agricul-

ture (corn, squash and beans, as in Mexico) was practiced and a kind of sun god was worshipped. Cahokia, the largest "city" north of Mexico before the Europeans arrived (five square miles), may possibly have been the capital of a centrally governed area.

Monk's Mound, the largest in North America, covers 16 acres and is 100 feet high. Debate still goes on concerning the extent of influence from the Mexican civilizations of the time.

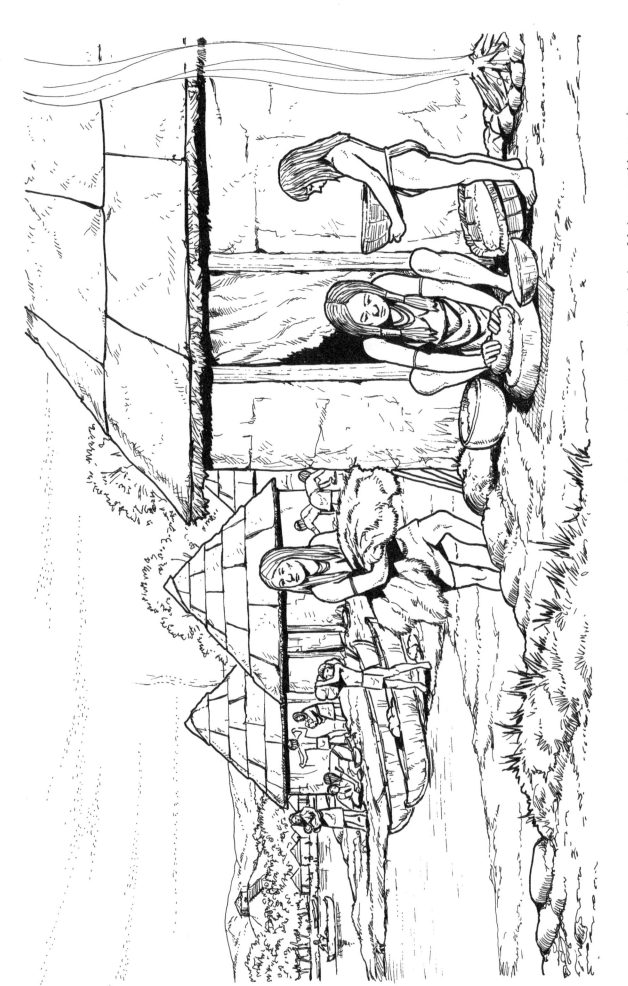

A village scene in the Mississippian period. It is clear from the monuments that there were many ranks in the society of the time, with wealth concentrated in the hands of a privileged few. Comparison with later cultures in the Mississippi valley leads many scholars to believe that there was a hierarchy of local chiefs owing allegiance to a paramount chief located at Cahokia. The chiefs may also have been the religious leaders of their communities, organizing the rites that were believed to be necessary for the proper growth of the crops. Mississippian influence went far beyond the immediate culture area, and villagers in many parts of North America were already combining agriculture with hunting.

Artistic products of the Norton culture, Alaska, about 500 A.D. The engraved ivory mask (above), which may originally have had a wooden backing, and the ivory object (below)—a comb?—are products of the Norton tradition from the coasts of the Bering Sea in Alaska (the western Arctic). The earliest Alaskan cultures (the Paleoarctic, about 8000 to 5000 B.C.) are mainly known from their rough stone tools. In the next phases (Kodiak tradition, Aleutian tradition, Arctic Small Tool tradition; down to about 800 B.C.) ocean fishing and hunting of marine mammals were practiced, finer and more varied stone tools were made, and the bow-and-arrow was introduced. The eastern Arctic regions of North America (eastern Canada and Greenland) were probably settled around 2000 B.C. In Alaska, the Small Tool culture was succeeded by the Norton period (down to about 800 A.D.), in which land hunting and river fishing became increasingly important and in which excellent art objects were produced.

Inuit hunters with kayak and dogsleds; the Thule tradition. New technology—the toggling harpoon and other hunting devices—introduced by inhabitants of islands in the Bering Strait about 700 B.C. began the so-called Thule tradition of the western Arctic, which lasted until modern times. Whale hunting now became possible. Kayaks like the one in the foreground have existed for about 2,000 years, and much of the hunting technology and gadgetry associated with the Inuit (Eskimo) was developed by 1000 A.D. In the eastern Arctic, the major culture was the Dorset tradition of about 550 B.C. to 1100 A.D.; spears and harpoons were used, but not the bow-and-arrow, and dogsleds were lacking. The Thule culture expanded into the eastern Arctic around 1000 A.D.

The ball court at Snaketown, Arizona, about 1100 A.D. One of the three or four major cultures of the "classic" (post-Archaic) period in the prehistoric Southwest was the Hohokam of the desert regions, about 400 to 1500 A.D. Maize agriculture and village life were introduced all over the Southwest early in this period. In the Hohokam area, villages were loose clusters of houses; there were already specialized large-scale pithouses, like the later ceremonial kivas. Multiroom buildings (proto-pueblos) arose in much of the Southwest between 700 and 1000 A.D., but the Hohokam maintained single-unit dwellings. The height of Hohokam civilization occurred at Snaketown, Arizona, from 900 to 1450 A.D. There were ball courts in which ceremonial matches like those in Mexico were held; platform mounds like those of the Mississippian culture were built; and extensive irrigation canals were dug. Trade networks extended from Tucson to Flagstaff.

Mogollon pithouse village in New Mexico, about 500 A.D. The Mogollon, another of the major classic Southwestern cultures, lasted from about 250 B.C. to 1450 A.D. in southeastern Arizona and southwestern New Mexico. The early pithouse villages were often situated defensively at the edges of mesas overlooking the valleys where the crops were grown. Later, villages occur in river valleys. There were ceremonial kivas, and certain larger houses may have belonged to community leaders. The leading artistic product was pottery, red-on-brown or polished red, which has been found over a large area, including Texas and northern Mexico.

Early Anasazi pit dwellings in Colorado, about 600 A.D. The most famous prehistoric Southwestern cultural group is the Anasazi (from the time of Christ to modern times) of the northerly regions, especially the "Four Corners." By the period 450–750, temporary brush and cave shelters had given way to houses partly dug into the ground (like earlier corn-storage pits) and partly continued above ground with poles and sticks daubed with adobe. Turkeys were domesticated, and the bow-and-arrow was introduced. Pottery began to replace baskets (early Anasazi phases used to be called "Basket-maker" by archaeologists).

Transitional Anasazi above-ground dwellings, about 800 A.D.
In this village scene of the period 750–900, the pole-and-adobe, or stone-and-adobe houses are above ground and abut each other, but they are not yet stacked, as in the later pueblos. The houses have both roof and door entrances. Ceremonial kivas were be- coming more elaborate. Types of settlements became much more varied in size and character, pointing to more complex social and political organization. By the end of this period, the Anasazi were ready for their peak development, in which they built some of the grandest pre-Columbian constructions in North America.

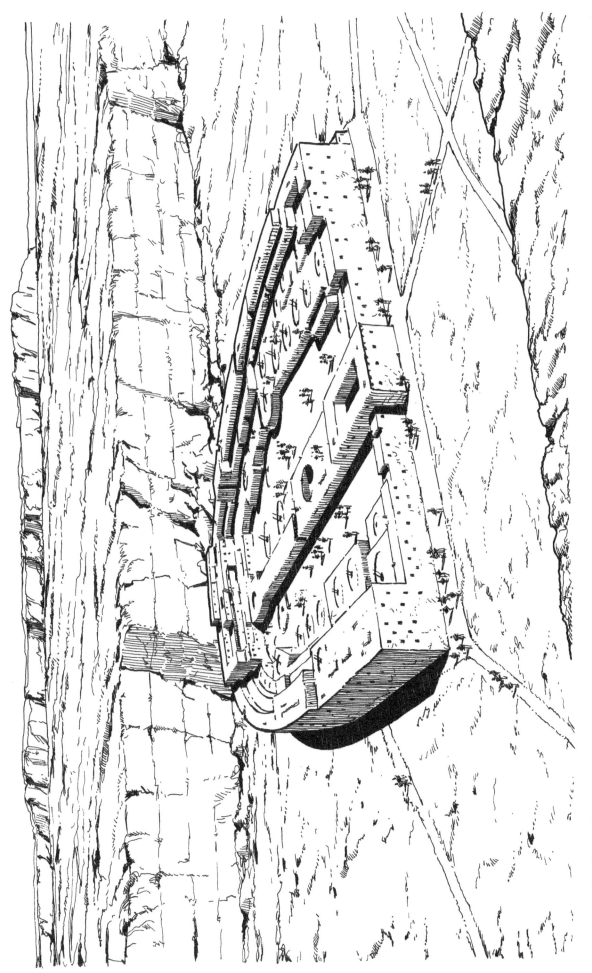

Pueblo Bonito, Chaco Canyon, northwestern New Mexico, about 1100 A.D. In the next Southwestern period, 900–1150, Chaco Canyon became the site of several Anasazi towns, interconnected by straight roads that extended up to 65 miles into the surrounding area. The largest town in the canyon was the three-acre Pueblo Bonito, built between about 900 and 1100 A.D. The outermost of its 800 or so rooms rose four or five stories high, forming a defensive perimeter. The dwelling places surrounded a plaza that was divided by another row of rooms, including the main kiva. The rise and collapse of the Chaco culture are subjects of much debate. Another important Southwestern culture, the Mimbres in southwestern New Mexico, flourished and disappeared within about the same time span. The Mimbres people are famed for their painted pottery, possibly the most beautiful North American pre-Columbian pieces.

Cliff Palace, Mesa Verde National Park, Colorado, about 1250 A.D. Between about 1200 and 1300 the Anasazi population in the Mesa Verde area peaked, and there were up to 1,000 cliff houses in what is now the national park. The largest and most impressive is Cliff Palace, the focus of the community, with 200 rooms and 23 ceremonial kivas. This pueblo, sheltered by a rock overhang, was abandoned, like its neighbors, at the end of the period. The people moved south and southeast to where the Hopi

and Zuñi live today. The Mesa Verde people probably had observatories and made calendars; they certainly cooperated on such community projects as water distribution. As the illustration indicates, they spent their waking hours outdoors whenever the weather permitted.

Deer hunters, Florida, 1560s. This illustration and the next two are based on drawings by Jacques Le Moyne, one of a group of Frenchmen who unsuccessfully tried to found a colony in Florida. In this view he recorded the Indians' practice of disguising themselves in deerskins in order to get close to living deer. These Indians were part of the Timucua confederation of northern Florida, who combined agriculture with hunting and gathering. Tall, wearing little clothing but elaborately tattooed, the Timucuan tribes lived in compact stockaded towns of circular houses built of poles and thatched with palmetto leaves. A special house for community gatherings stood in the center.

Ceremonies before going on the warpath, Florida, 1560s. The Timucua chiefs enjoyed great authority; the people were warlike and well organized militarily. They practiced scalping, human sacrifice and perhaps cannibalism. In this scene a chief worships the sun with a wooden platter of water he has scooped from one of the large containers; he will now sprinkle his warriors with the water, praying that their enemies' blood will be spilled likewise. The Timucua people were converted to Christianity by the Spanish who had followed up Ponce de León's discovery. Many of them died of diseases introduced by the Europeans; most of the rest were killed in the 17th and 18th centuries by tribes controlled by the English colonists who had settled north of Florida.

Panning for gold, Appalachians, 1560s. The Timucua people told their French guests that the rivers of the Appalachian Mountains contained gold, silver and other minerals. The local natives dug collection ditches in the streams. Other local activities recorded by the artist Le Moyne included: the funeral of a chief, a shaman's performance, the smoking of meat on racks, the mode of killing alligators, the dedication of a deerskin to the sun, a chief's wedding procession, a council, the sowing of a field, care of the sick, preparations for a feast and various sports. His series of drawings is one of the finest monuments to an "unspoiled" Native American group and our chief source of knowledge on the particular subject.

Choctaw "lacrosse" game. The Choctaw lived in southeastern Mississippi before being forced to move to Oklahoma in the 1830s (along with the Creek, Cherokee and Chickasaw). Living in mud-covered log or bark cabins in well-organized villages, they were the best farmers in the Southeast, growing corn, beans, squash and sunflowers. They and several other tribes played a popular spectator game somewhat like lacrosse on a large field with goalposts at either end. Each team had up to 100 players, and the confrontation was extremely violent. Dancing and other ceremonies, and much betting, preceded the games. The illustration is based on paintings by George Catlin, who visited the Choctaw in Mississippi.

Green Corn Rite of the Creek. Southeastern Indian religion was closely connected with agriculture and the growth cycle of cultivated plants. The chief holy day was the Busk, or Green Corn Rite, a four-day new-year celebration held late in the summer when the corn ripened. The first day was spent cleaning homes and the council house; the second day, feasting; the third day, fasting. On the fourth day, a new sacred fire was lit outdoors, and elderly men and women, carrying branches and wearing leg rattles of shell, danced around it. The Creek lived in parts of Georgia and Alabama. The women did most of the farming. Their houses and villages were, in general, similar to the Choctaws'. Some towns had a thatched dome-shaped temple on top of a mound.

Natchez royal funeral. The highest level of Southeastern civilization still extant when the Europeans arrived was achieved by the Natchez in Mississippi, near the present city of that name. They depended chiefly on agriculture, and were very skilled in textiles (mulberry-bark clothing), pottery and other arts. Their head chief had more power than any other in the Southeast, and their sun-worshipping religion was the most advanced; their religious architecture and practices point to a strong lasting influence from the Mississippi tradition (see pages 14–16). In the illustration, the mother of a head chief and her husband, who has been killed to join her in the other world, are being carried on a bier to the temple mound in a procession led by the high priest (on the steps). The chief is at the top of the staircase. The dead woman's house is being burned. The Natchez were dispersed by 1800, after several wars against the French.

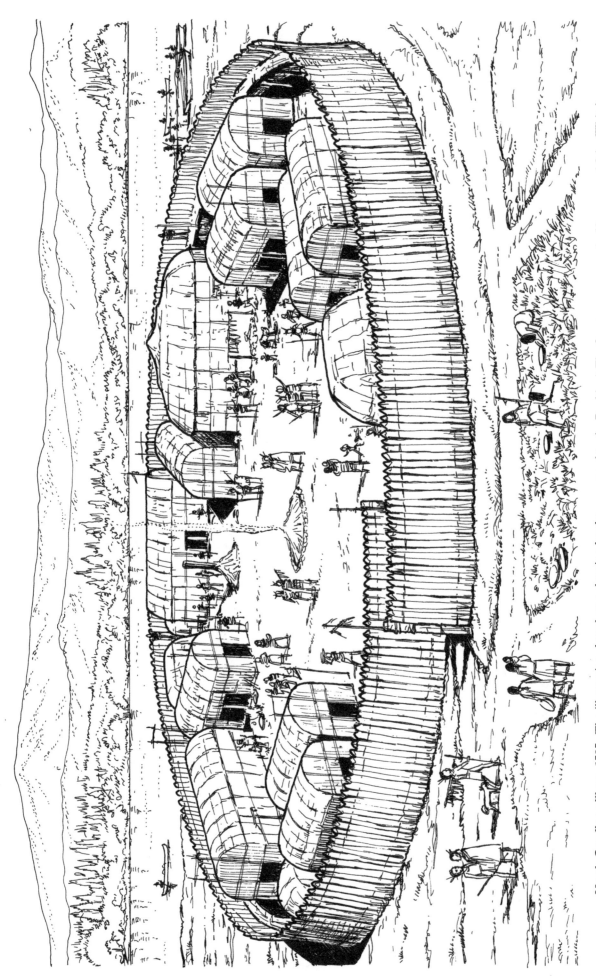

North Carolina village, 1585. The illustration, based on a drawing by the Englishman John White, one of the Roanoke colonists (the first English colony in the New World), shows the Secotan tribe village of Pomeiooc, a typical palisaded settlement of those Algonquian Indians who inhabited the middle Atlantic coast of the future U.S. (Other speakers of Algonquian languages lived in Canada, New England, the Great Lakes region and west-ward to the Rockies.) The Secotan were gone in 50 years, and John White's record is as important in their regard as Le Moyne's for the Timucua (pages 26–28). Middle-Atlantic Algonquians, such as the Delaware and Powhatan, worshiped the Great Spirit, who symbolized the forces of nature; they fished, hunted and planted corn and tobacco. They painted their bodies and wore little clothing.

River camp of Northeastern Algonquians. Algonquian-speaking tribes of the Northeast included the Micmac, Penobscot, Passamaquoddy, Abnaki, Montauk, Pequot, Narragansett and many others. They hunted moose; trapped beaver; fished with spears, weirs and nets; lived seminomadically in portable wigwams of saplings covered with bark; and wore animal-skin clothing. This river-camp scene illustrates many features of their everyday life: (left to right) birchbark canoes, a woman treating skins, a fisherman with his catch, a woman finger-weaving a robe, an elm-bark wigwam, a woman grinding corn in a wooden mortar, and a baby in a cradleboard hung on a birch tree.

Inside an Iroquois longhouse. In the broad sense, the name Iroquois applies to all speakers of Iroquoian languages (in many parts of the Great Lakes and east coast); in the narrower sense, to the upper New York State groups who joined together in the Iroquois League about 1600 A.D. The New York State Iroquois were noted for their longhouses of poles and bark, 50-to-150-foot dwellings for a number of families of the same lineage (the individual family compartments could be curtained off). The women did the farming while the men, in bands, did the building, hunting, trading and fighting. There were agricultural festivals reminiscent of those in the Southeast.

Iroquois False Face ceremony. The Iroquois were highly organized socially. Council meetings for mutual decisions occupied much of the men's time, and oratory was an important achievement. There were also religious societies, of which the False Face group is the most famous; wearing bizarre wooden masks and wielding turtle-shell rattles, the members would perform curing rituals for a fee. One area in which mutual decisions were not sufficiently binding was warfare. Martial glory was so important to the young men that they often flouted the wisdom of their elders and went on the warpath on their own. So many were killed that sometimes captives were adopted to maintain the tribe's manpower level.

Huron dance to cure sickness, 1620. The Hurons of the St. Lawrence River region spoke an Iroquoian language, and their way of life was similar to that of the League Iroquois, but the latter were their bitterest enemies. Among the Huron, farming was more important than hunting. Great attention was given to ceremonies for the dead. Women were more influential in politics than with the League Iroquois. The illustration, which depicts a dancing ceremony to cure illness (led by the shaman, or medicine man), is based on an engraving in a book by the French explorer Samuel de Champlain. The Huron confederacy was finally destroyed by the Iroquois League around 1650; those Hurons who were captured had to live with the Iroquois, the others were dispersed in different directions.

The Great Lakes area: harvesting wild rice. The westernmost Woodland Indians were those of the Great Lakes area, including such Algonquian-speaking tribes as the Menominee, Potawatomi, Ottawa, Ojibwa, Fox and Sauk, and the Siouan-speaking Winnebago. All these tribes combined farming with hunting; most of them hunted buffalo. Favorite foodstuffs included maple sugar, tapped in early spring, and wild rice (the grain of a wild-growing aquatic grass), gathered in summertime. The illustration is based on a drawing by the 19th-century American artist Seth Eastman.

The Great Lakes area: a Midewiwin Society rite. The summer was always a period of ceremonies in honor of the supernatural forces of nature, but the nature of the rites changed with time. Around 1600 the Midewiwin, or Grand Medicine Society, was the most popular in the region. The purpose was to cure illness and gain immortality for the soul. Other religious practices of the Great Lakes area were the smoking of the calumet ("peace pipe") on ceremonial occasions, and the vision quest, in which teenage boys fasted until they dreamed of the personal guardian spirit that would help them become good hunters and fighters.

The Southern Plains: a Comanche tepee village in Texas.
Based on an 1834 painting by George Catlin, this illustration includes one animal that was missing from the scene for most of the pre-Columbian millennia: the horse, reintroduced to the New World by the Spanish in the early 16th century. Horses (and rifles) revolutionized the hunting of buffalo, which had been the main prey of Plains Indians since time immemorial, and their chief source of food, clothing, shelter and fuel. The Plains tribes encountered by the Europeans had moved there relatively recently, and the restless movements went on long after first discovery. The heyday of the Comanche was around 1800; they had extensive and complex trade relationships with Spanish settlements, and they also raided widely, even deep into Mexico.

The Central Plains: outdoor occupations in a village. The tribes of the Central Plains (Pawnee, Dakota, Arapaho, Cheyenne, etc.) are the most famous of all North American Indian groups, and their buffalo-hide tepees are a symbol of Indian life in general. In this scene we see a hunter with his dog, a woman cooking stew in a buffalo-paunch "pot," another woman with a child in a Sioux-type cradleboard, and yet another woman preparing rawhide (scraping and smoothing a pegged-down buffalo hide) for saddlebags. The life style of the various Central Plains peoples was quite similar. Their spoken languages might be very different, but they all understood a common sign language that could express simple, basic ideas and wishes.

The Northern Plains: the Okipa ceremony of the Mandan.
Northern Plains tribes included the Blackfoot, Cree, Gros Ventre, Assiniboin, Hidatsa and Mandan. The Mandan were peaceful farmers and tracers who were wiped out by smallpox in the first half of the 19th century—fortunately not before being visited by the artists George Catlin and Karl Bodmer, who left us priceless records of the tribe's existence. Mandan villages consisted of lodges with domed earth roofs arranged around a plaza. Among their numerous colorful ceremonies was the four-day summertime Okipa honoring the mythical origins of the tribe; the young men endured ordeals similar to those in the Central Plains Sun Dance, including a wild race around the central post of the plaza, with buffalo skulls tied to them.

The Great Basin: a Paiute encampment. The tribes of the Great Basin (Utah, Nevada and parts of adjacent states) included the Ute, Paiute and Shoshoni. Life was hard in this parched environment, and the Indians had to wander incessantly for water and food (fish, berries, piñon nuts, eggs, rabbits, etc.). Camps were temporary and simple; the Paiutes built conical huts (wickiups) of willow poles covered with brush or reeds. Basketweaving was an important activity on which much skill was lavished. Sacajawea, the famous guide of Lewis and Clark, was a Shoshoni woman. Old petroglyphs (drawings and designs chipped out of boulders) have been found in the Great Basin area.

The Southwest: Hopi Snake Ceremonial. The multistory hilltop pueblos of the corn-growing, sheep-raising descendants of the Anasazi (see pages 21–25) are known internationally, as are their magnificent basketry, pottery, kachina dolls and turquoise-and-silver jewelry. Their mythology is extremely elaborate, and their ceremonies are some of the most striking anywhere. The Hopi Snake Ceremonial, performed in late August to bring rain, lasts nine days. On the ninth day, the Snake Society members, wearing special feather headgear and skirts, take live snakes, some poisonous, from their temporary enclosure and dance around the plaza, each man with a snake in his mouth and accompanied by a guard (the guards hold eagle feathers to stroke the snake with to prevent it from biting). Afterwards, the snakes are returned unharmed to the desert.

The Southwest: scene in a kiva. As mentioned on pages 19, 22 and 23, the underground ceremonial pit known as the kiva goes far back in Southwest history. Its shape and structure are like those of the oldest Anasazi dwellings. For the modern Pueblo peoples, it represents the lower world from which man once emerged. It is used as a clubhouse, a meetingplace for councils and a religious center. Women are almost never allowed in. The bright paintings on kiva walls may represent either mythological events or scenes from everyday life. Since Pueblo communities include at least two clans, and the kivas are connected with clans, there are at least two kivas in every village.

California: Chumash village scene. When the Europeans arrived, there were about 300,000 Indians in California, living in small, independent groups, and speaking over 100 different languages and dialects. Village life had not significantly progressed beyond the Archaic hunting-and-gathering stage (see pages 8 and 10). The illustration shows some of the magnificent basketry for which the Californians are famous. The fish indicate the special skills of the coastal Chumash tribe (from the area around Malibu) as fishermen, using 25-foot canoes of driftwood or pine planks. They also gathered shellfish and hunted seals for their skins. Other California Indians made similarly effective use of their immediate environment.

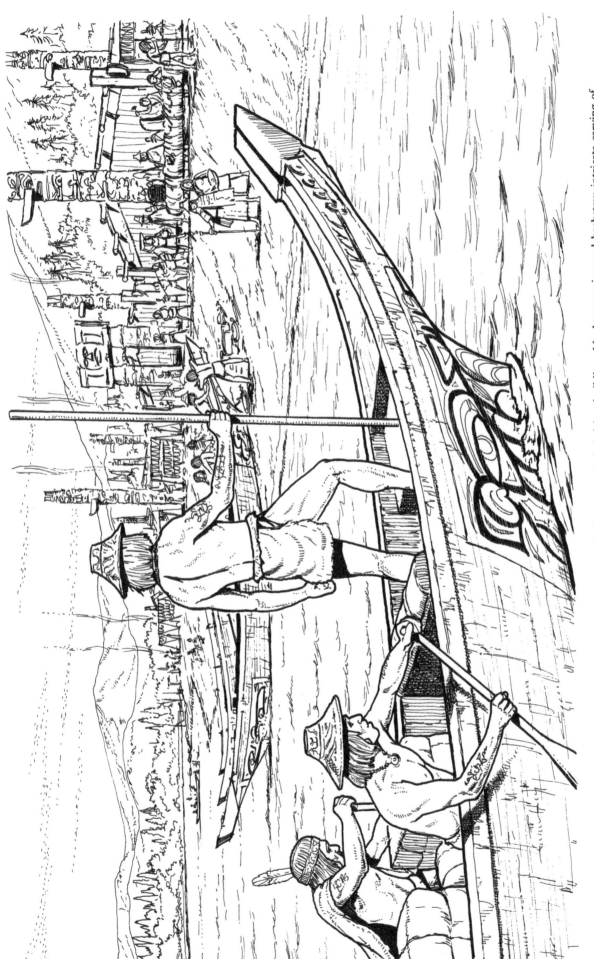

Northwest Coast village scene. The forest and the ocean regulated the lives of these tribes (Tsimshian, Haida, Chinook, Kwakiutl, Tlingit, etc.). Their villages, ranging from 50 to 1,000 inhabitants, were distinguished by cedar-plank houses in front of which were tall posts ("totem poles") carved with mythical beings representing the mythological history of the family. Their arts included boatbuilding, blanket weaving and basketry; intricate carving of furniture, pipes and masks; and bold, symmetrical decorative painting. River salmon fishing, deepsea fishing and whaling were major activities. Dramatic performances of myths formed a striking element in their culture.

The Northwest Coast: a potlatch feast. The Northwest Coast environment provided so much food that the people did not have to spend all their time gathering it (as in many other areas); they had time for trade and the accumulation of personal wealth. At potlatch feasts, which occurred in no other pre-Columbian region, wealthy members of one clan would honor another clan by offering huge amounts of food and bestowing enormous numbers of gifts. Both hosts and guests were clothed in expensive finery. In the illustration, the standing man closest to the center is carrying a piece of engraved metal (a "copper"), which will be the chief gift. The raven-masked man will perform a clan legend. A potlatch might require years of preparation and might last more than ten days.

The Subarctic: Kutchin hunters in winter houses, Yukon, Canada. The Arctic regions, until very recent times, remained basically as they had been for hundreds of years (see pages 17 and 18). The Subarctic, covering most of Canada and parts of Alaska (representative tribes: Naskapi, Chipewyan, Dogrib, Kutchin), was a cold world of tundra and evergreen forest. Like the buffalo on the Plains, the staff of life was the caribou (New World reindeer), whose extensive migrations were carefully studied and exploited; hunting was usually a cooperative endeavor. The Kutchins were one of the Athabascan-speaking tribes of the west; nomads, they built lightweight, domed temporary houses of poles and caribou hide, which could be struck like tents and carried on sleds. The raised platform in the background of the picture was for food storage.